THE CHURCH MINISTRY CLIP ART BOOK is your source for wonderful art, borders, Bible verses and more to spice up your ministry's publications. In an effort to make your job as easy as possible, we've kept all our instructions and suggestions simple and straightforward—there's nothing here that even a nervous first-time user can't easily master. So sit back, relax, and let your own creativity and the contents of this book unleash some terrific handbills, Sunday bulletins, mail outs, and posters!

■ CONTENTS ■

HOW TO USE THE CHURCH MINISTRY CLIP ART BOOK ▬▬●

THE TOOLS AND SUPPLIES REQUIRED:

- Rubber cement
- Scissors and/or X-Acto knife with #11 blades
- Typewriter and paper
- Cardstock for paste-up
- Art from this book

Optional:

- Transfer (rub-on or peel-and-stick) letters and numbers

Transfer letters are great for making special headlines. Buy them at any good art supply store. The manufacturers' catalogs have complete instructions.

ääääåååååàààààaabb"
bbbcccccccccdddddddd
dèèèèèèèèèèèèééééé"
'éèèèèèèèffffffggggg'
ghhhhhhhhhhhhhhhiiii
iiiiiiiiiijjjjkkkkkkll
lllllllllllmmmmmmmm

PREPARING ARTWORK FOR PUBLICATION

1. Cut out the artwork and glue it to the cardstock.

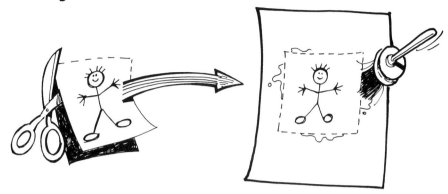

2. Use the headlines in this book, or create your own.

3. Type your message on another piece of paper and glue it to the cardstock.

4. Run off as many copies as you need. There, that wasn't so bad!

THE CHURCH MINISTRY CLIP ART BOOK

Featuring the artwork of

Gustave Dore

Tom Finley

Barbara Fisher

Elaine Godinez

Dennis Jones

Jack Kershner

Ted Killian

Bron Smith

Wendy Talbot

Sherilee Williams

CHURCH MINISTRIES CLIP ART ▉

This section contains illustrations for just about every ministry and activity your church could sponsor. Sometimes it was hard for us to decide what art to put under which heading. For example, should singing go under Music or Worship? Keep in mind that art you can't find under one heading may be under another. Make a habit of using the detailed Table of Contents on pages 4 and 5.

Every illustration is reproduced in more that one size for your convenience. Each page is blank on the back so artwork can be clipped out without ruining art on the reverse side. The pages are perforated for easy removal. The book is three hole punched so loose pages may be stored in a binder.

Christian Education ▉

Bible Study

Bible Study

Bible Study

Bible Study

Bible Study

Bible Study

Bible Study

Bible Talk Study Group

Bible Talk Study Group

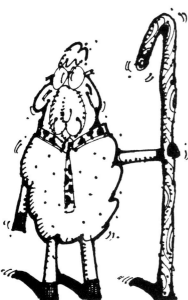

Discipleship

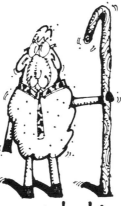

Discipleship

God's Word

God's Word

• Group Discussion Class

Group Discussion Class

" PANEL DISCUSSION "
OR
" SPECIAL COMMITTEE "

" PANEL DISCUSSION "
OR
" SPECIAL COMMITTEE "

PRAYER GROUP

• PRAYER GROUP

PRAYER GROUP

Prayer Meeting

Prayer Meeting   Prayer Meeting

• *Pastor's Notes:*   *Pastor's Notes:*

A CALL FOR
VOLUNTEERS

A CALL FOR
VOLUNTEERS

TEACH

TEACH

TEACHERS NEEDED
FOR ALL AGES

TEACHERS NEEDED
FOR ALL AGES

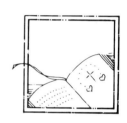

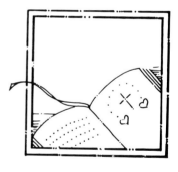

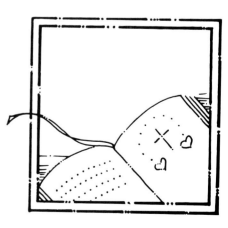

14

15

16

CLOWN

MINISTRY

DAYCARE NURSERY PROVIDED

DAYCARE NURSERY PROVIDED

New Babies!
New Babies!

NURSERY CLASS AGES 0-2

VOLUNTEERS NEEDED

POLY SIGH...

Single/Young Marrieds

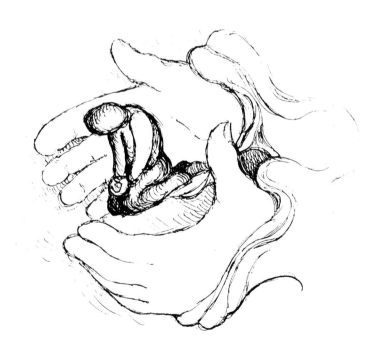

DIVORCE

DIVORCE

.MARRIAGE
COUNSELING

MARRIAGE ENRICHMENT
MARRIAGE ENRICHMENT
MARRIAGE ENRICHMENT

Family Ministry *Family Ministry*

Seniors

Worship/Fellowship

FELLOWSHIP NITE

Communion
Communion
Fellowship
Fellowship

FELLOWSHIP NITE

FELLOWSHIP NITE

Praise Him!

Praise Him!

Worship

Worship

Singing and Praise!

Singing and Praise!

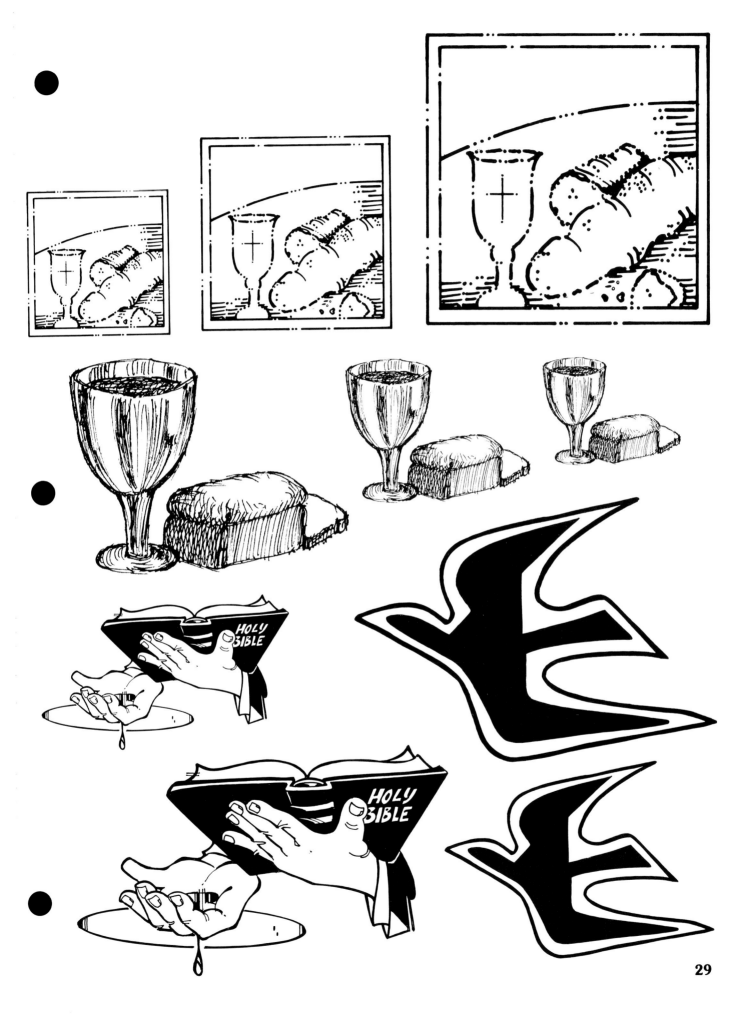

29

Evangelism/ Visitation/Missions

Evangelism

Evangelism

WELCOME

WELCOME

WELCOME

Missions

Missions Missions

Missions Missions

PHILIPPI
ASIA
BEREA
TROAS
MACEDONIA
EPHESUS
TO SYRIA AND JERUSALEM
MILETU
GREECE

PHILIPPI
ASIA
BEREA
TROAS
MACEDONIA
EPHESUS
TO SYRIA AND JERUSALEM
MILETU
GREECE

Social Concern

INADEQUATE HOUSING

COMMUNITY DEVELOPMENT CRISIS!

INADEQUATE HOUSING

COMMUNITY DEVELOPMENT CRISIS!

INADEQUATE HOUSING

COMMUNITY DEVELOPMENT CRISIS!

33

JAIL MINISTRY

Toy Drive for Needy Children's Home

JAIL MINISTRY

SHOW YOU CARE!

Calendar

CALENDAR

CALENDAR   Calendar

CALENDAR   Calendar

January February March April May June July August September October November December

Saturday
Sunday
Monday
Tuesday
Wednesday
Thursday
Friday

SCHEDULE

SCHEDULE

Schedule *Schedule* *Schedule*

This Month

This Month *This Month*

This Week

This Week *This Week*

Seasons/Holidays

Fall

Summer

Winter

Spring

Fall

Summer

Winter

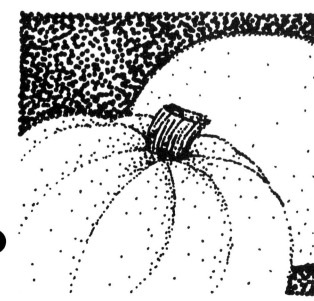

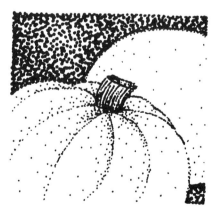

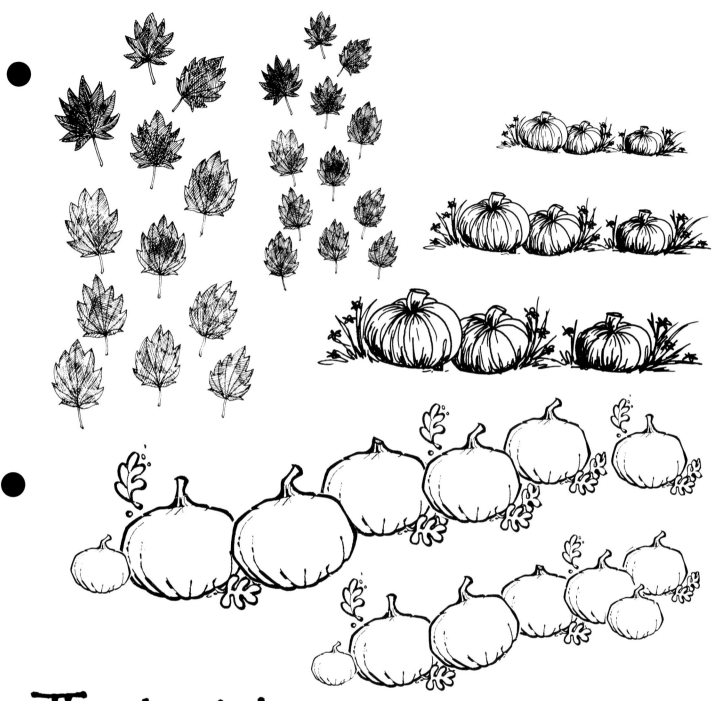

Thanksgiving

Thanksgiving

Christmas Boutique

Christmas Party

Christmas Party

A Christmas Party

Holiday Program

Holy Night

Holiday Program

Holy Night

Seasons Greetings

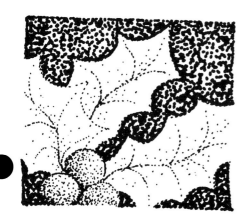

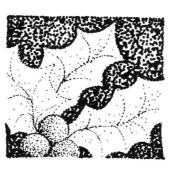

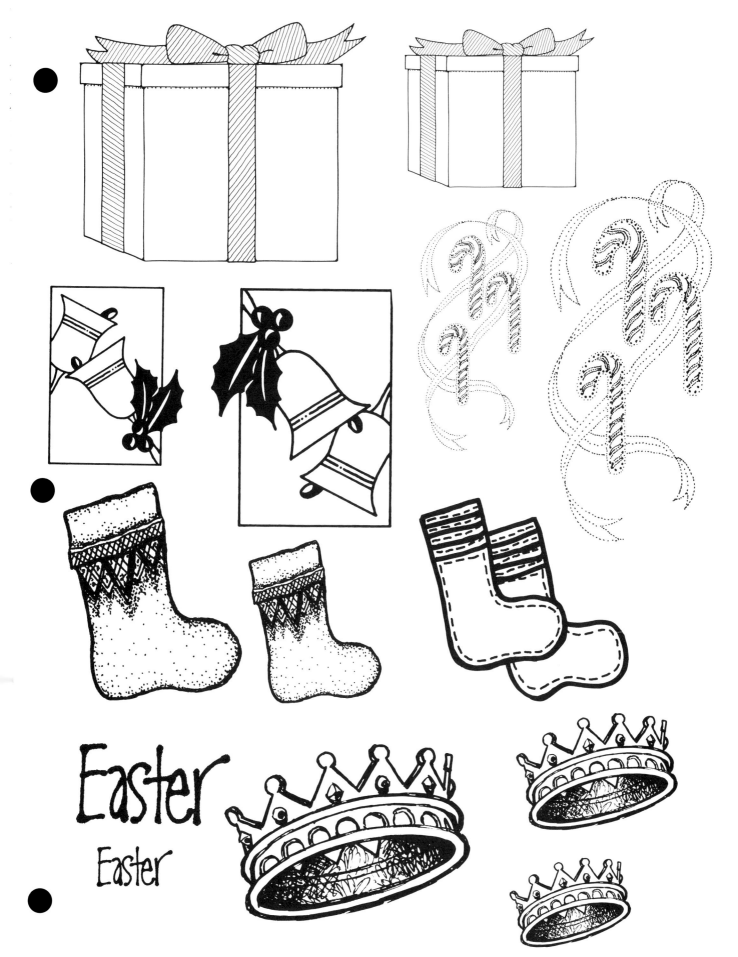

Easter

Easter

Love

Sacrifice

Glory

Music

More than Music...

More than Music...

You shall **LOVE** THE LORD, YOUR **GOD** with all your heart and with all your soul and with all your mind. Deut. 6:5

You shall **LOVE** THE LORD, YOUR **GOD** with all your heart and with all your soul and with all your mind. Deut. 6:5

You shall **LOVE** THE LORD, YOUR **GOD** with all your heart and with all your soul and with all your mind. Deut. 6:5

... i have hidden your word in my heart... Ps. 119:11 (NIV)

... i have hidden your word in my heart.. Ps. 119:11 (NIV)

... i have hidden your word in my heart.. Ps. 119:11 (NIV)

Blessed are those who have been persecuted for the sake of righteous, for theirs is the kingdom of heaven. Matt. 5:10

Blessed are those who have been persecuted for the sake of righteous, for theirs is the kingdom of heaven. Matt. 5:10

COME TO ME ALL WHO ARE WEARY AND HEAVY-LADEN AND I WILL GIVE YOU **Rest** Matt. 11:28

COME TO ME ALL WHO ARE WEARY AND HEAVY-LADEN AND I WILL GIVE YOU **Rest** Matt. 11:28

COME TO ME ALL WHO ARE WEARY AND HEAVY-LADEN AND I WILL GIVE YOU **Rest** Matt. 11:28

BE ON YOUR GUARD
STAND FAST IN THE FAITH
BE MEN OF COURAGE, BE STRONG
DO EVERYTHING IN LOVE

1 CORINTHIANS 16:13,14

WATCH YE. STAND
FAST IN THE FAITH. QUIT YOU LIKE MEN.
BE STRONG. LET ALL YOUR THINGS BE
DONE WITH CHARITY.

1 CORINTHIANS 16:13,14

BE ON YOUR GUARD
STAND FAST IN THE FAITH
BE MEN OF COURAGE, BE STRONG
DO EVERYTHING IN LOVE

1 CORINTHIANS 16:13,14

WATCH YE. STAND
FAST IN THE FAITH. QUIT YOU LIKE MEN.
BE STRONG. LET ALL YOUR THINGS BE
DONE WITH CHARITY.

1 CORINTHIANS 16:13,14

LOVE JOY! PEACE patience KINDNESS goodness faithfulness gentleness SELF-CONTROL

BIBLE VERSE TO MEMORIZE

LOVE
JOY!
PEACE
PATIENCE
KINDNESS
goodness
SELF-CONTROL
GENTLENESS
faithfulness

"Don't worry about anything= instead pray about everything= tell God your needs and don't forget to thank Him for His answers." Philippians 4:6

"Don't worry about anything= instead pray about everything= tell God your needs and don't forget to thank Him for His answers." Philippians 4:6

"My God shall supply all your needs according to His riches in glory in Christ Jesus." Philippians 4:19

"My God shall supply all your needs according to His riches in glory in Christ Jesus." Philippians 4:19

52

MEN'S COFFEE HOUR

MEN'S COFFEE HOUR

COFFEE KLATCH

COFFEE KLATCH

COFFEE TIME

COFFEE TIME

WE'LL SEE YOU AT THE CHURCH PICNIC!

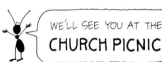

WE'LL SEE YOU AT THE CHURCH PICNIC!

WE'LL SEE YOU AT THE CHURCH PICNIC!

Donut Time!
Donut Time!

54

Eats! Eats!

FLAPJACK FEED

Picnic!

Picnic!

FLAPJACK FEED

Potluck Supper

Potluck Supper

Spring Banquet

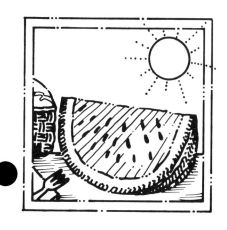

55

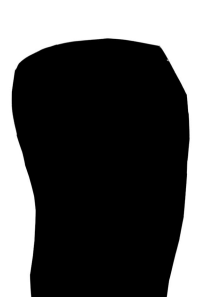

People/Bible People

57

58

 Come and Get It !

 Come and Get It !

 Come and Get It !

 Computer Games

 Computer Games

Day in the Park

FUND DRIVE

He Is The Light

He Is The Light

HURRY TO THE

HURRY TO THE

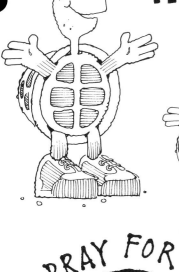

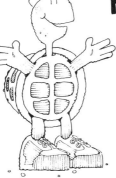

•REPORT

REPORT REPORT

See You There!

SERVANTS'
ENTRANCE

• Suffering dishonesty the rap
       bruises sin Welts
          wrongdoing

64

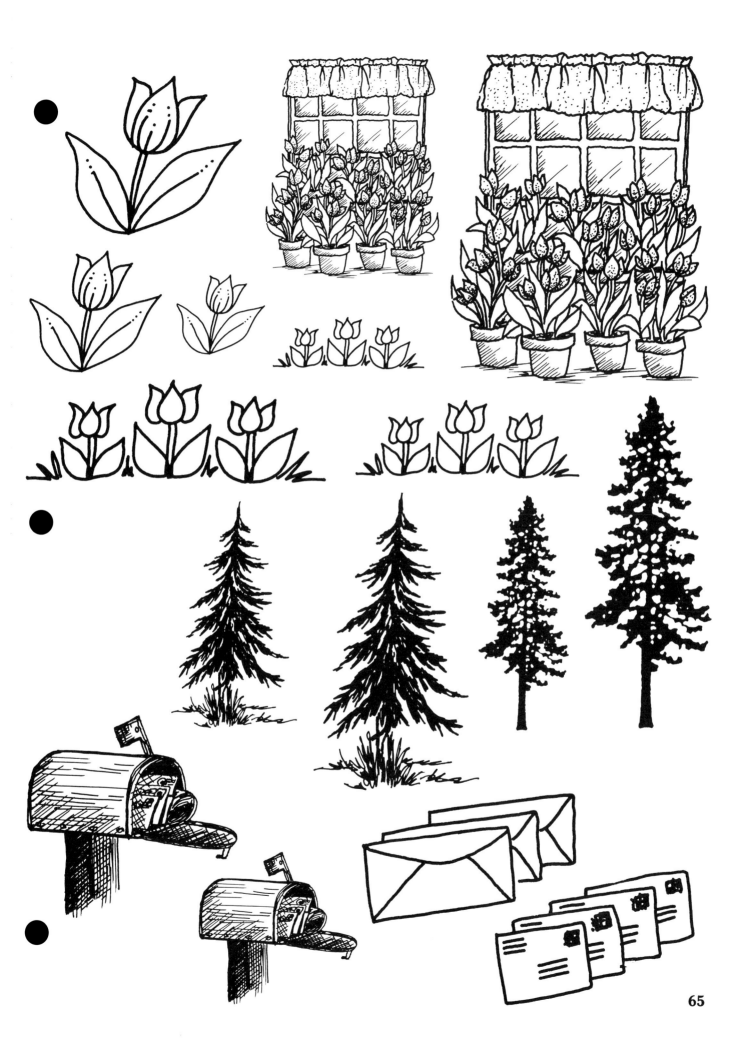

65

Open Home *Open Home*

Castles in the Sand

Castles in the Sand

BANNERS AND BORDERS

Use these to add emphasis to your printed product's most important notes and messages.

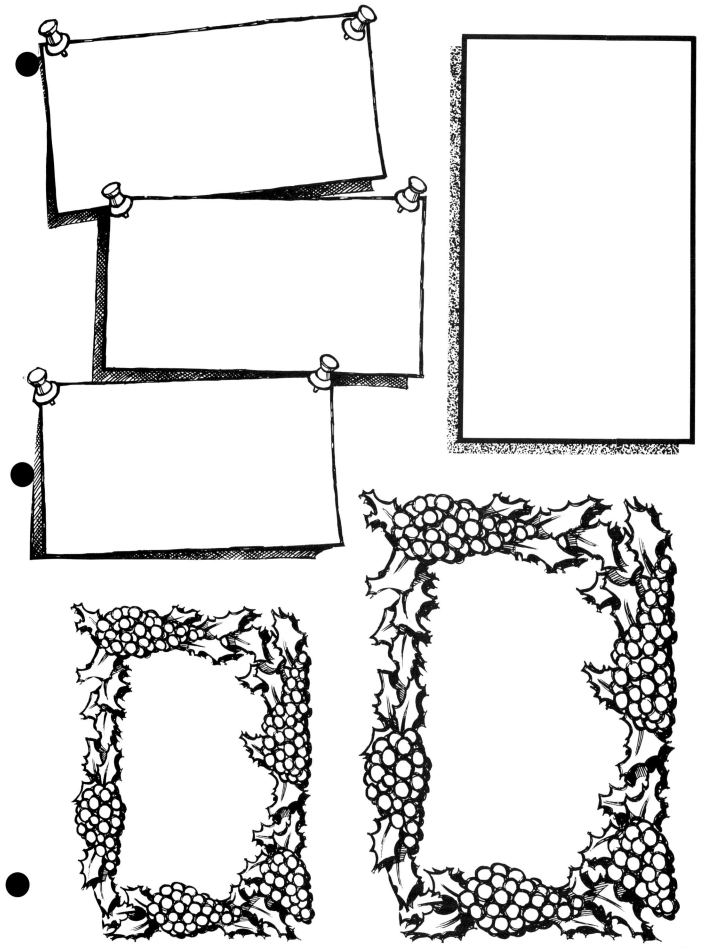

72

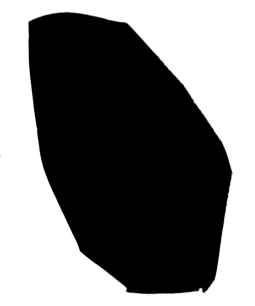

77

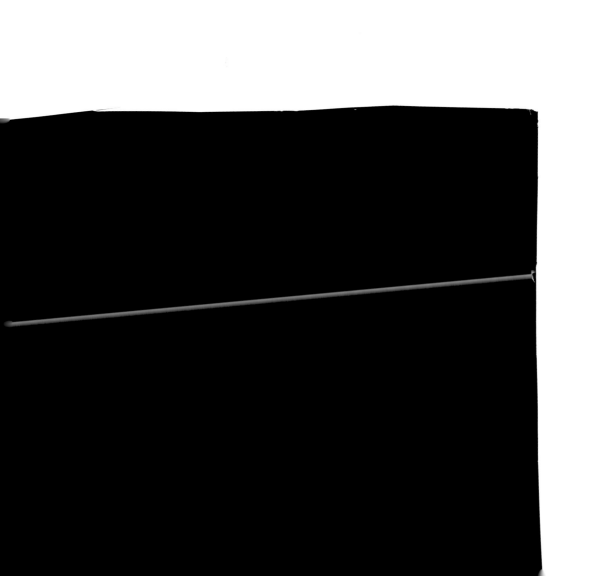

FATHER ➡ SON ➡ HOLY SPIRIT ➡ CHRISTIAN

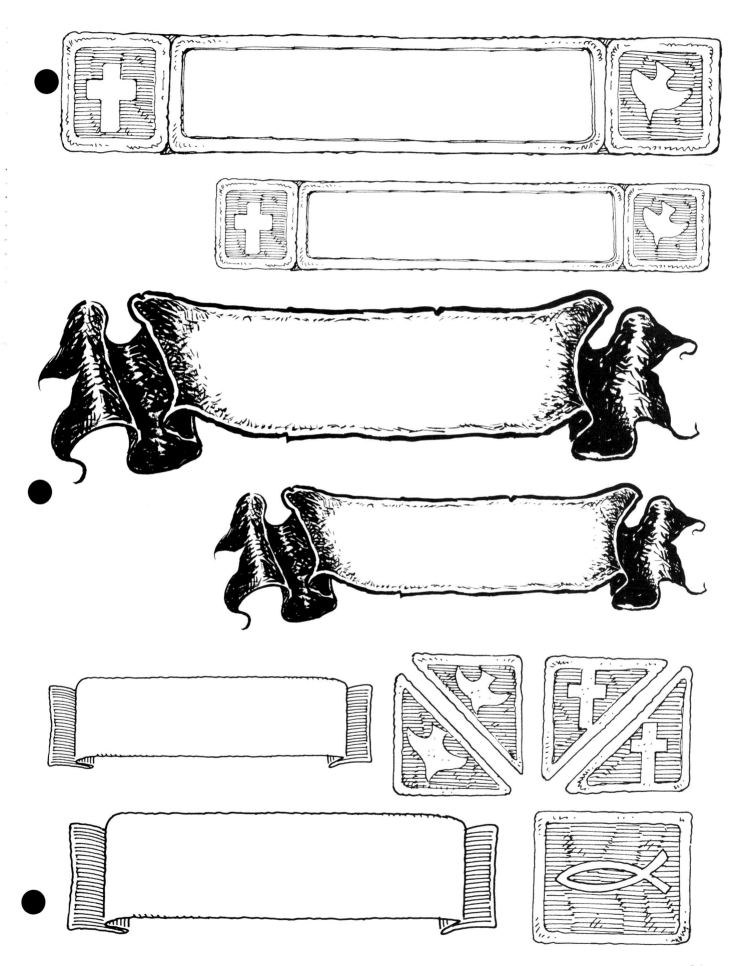

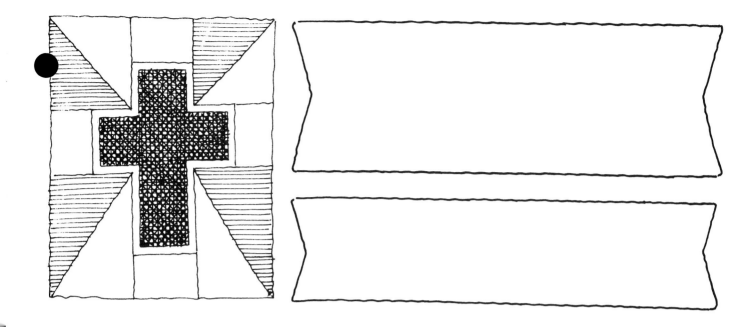

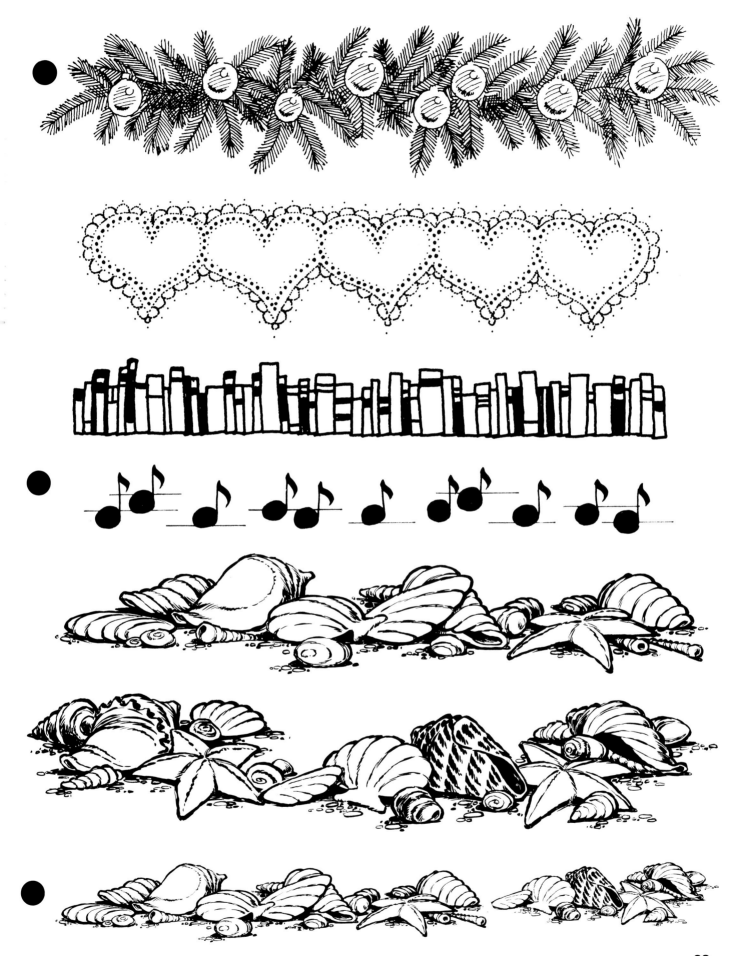

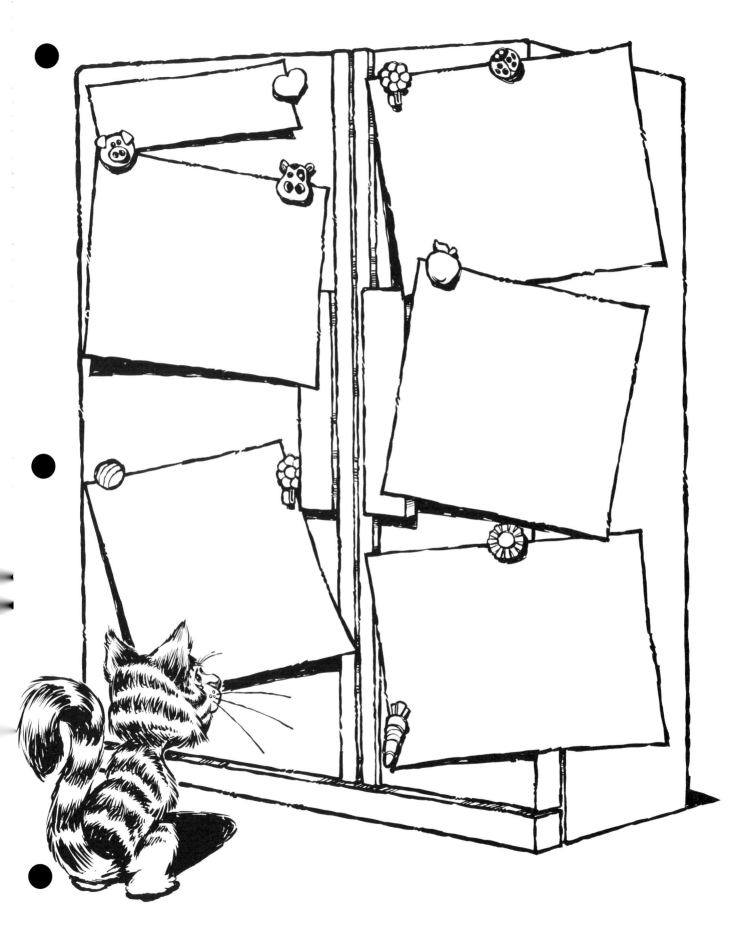

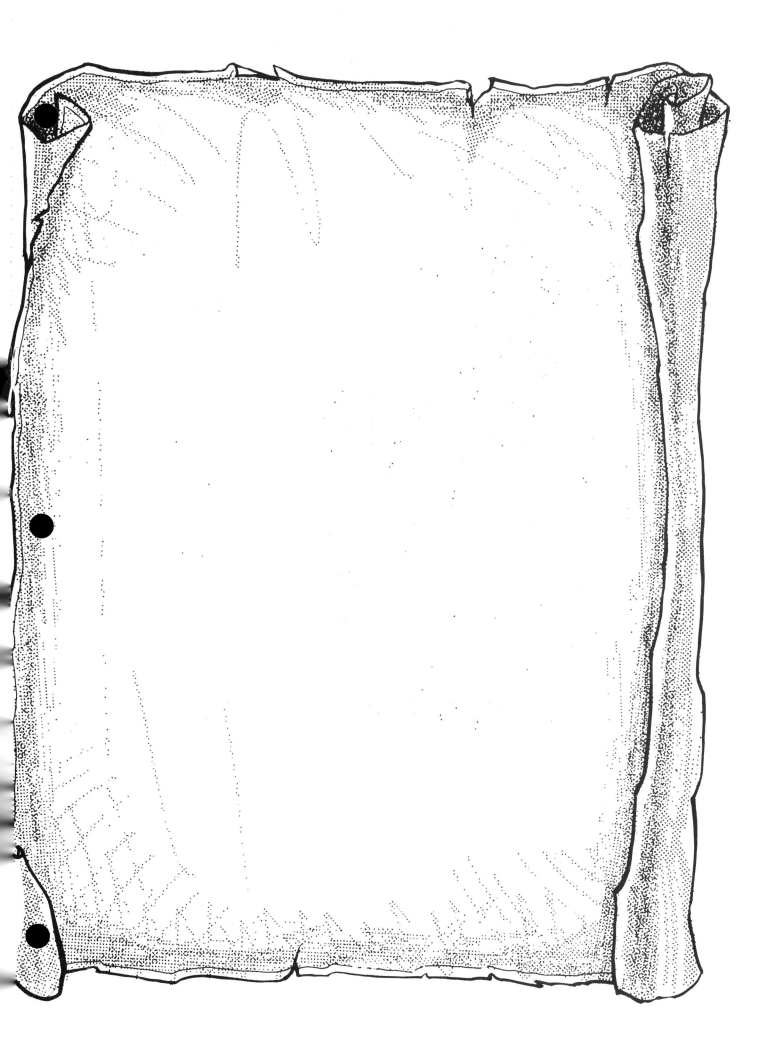

DORE PLATES

The Holy Bible, with Illustrations by Gustave Dore was first published in 1865. Dore created 241 plates for the Bible, and his achievement stands as one of the highest accomplishments in religious art.

BUILDING FUND

OTHER CLIP ART BOOKS FROM GOSPEL LIGHT

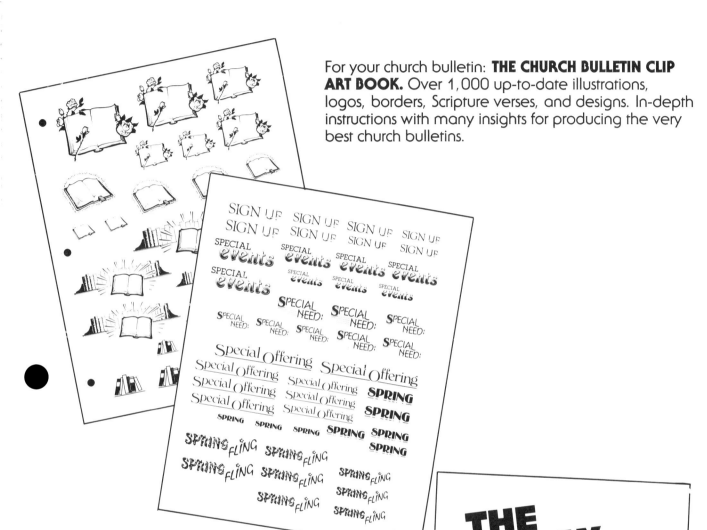

For your church bulletin: **THE CHURCH BULLETIN CLIP ART BOOK.** Over 1,000 up-to-date illustrations, logos, borders, Scripture verses, and designs. In-depth instructions with many insights for producing the very best church bulletins.

For your children's ministry: **THE SUNDAY SCHOOL CLIP ART BOOK.** An invaluable aid for putting together class worksheets, announcements to parents, and much more. Hundreds of illustrations, borders and designs by professional Christian artists.

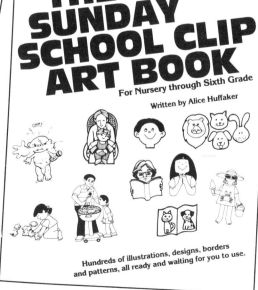

For your youth group: The original **YOUTH WORKER'S CLIP ART BOOK, SON OF CLIP ART** and **I WAS A TEENAGE CLIP ART BOOK.** Clip art by youth workers for youth workers. Create terrific monthly mail outs, handbills, classroom worksheets and overhead transparencies. Special features include Bible games, short stories, greeting cards and brain teasers.

You can obtain these truly helpful resources from your Christian supplier, or call Gospel Light toll free 1-800 235-3415 (outside California) or 1-800 227-4025 (California only).